Anti-Inflammatory Recipes Based on GAPS Nutrient-Dense Protocol

Healing Leaky Gut Recipes

Gut and Psycology Syndrome

Ketogenic

Paleolithic

SIBO/FODMAP

Weston A Price Foundation

Nakisa Nowroozi, PhD

Foreword:

It is with the greatest pleasure that I am able to introduce you to Nakisa Nowroozi and her new book of GAPS-inspired recipes.

Nakisa came to me in 2015 with questions about healing her son's stomach problems, allergies and eczema. She had found the GAPS Diet (Gut and Psychology Syndrome) and through that me, a GAPS Practitioner.

Nakisa was the perfect client, dutifully following all the GAPS guidelines, which includes spending quite a bit of time in the kitchen. She did not put this time to waste! Nakisa got creative, drew on her family's traditional foods, and continued to impress me with the variety and delicious sounding meals she made for her son and family.

Today her son is healthy and happy, and she is sharing her recipes with all of us.

Step away from the usual sweet potato fries and meatballs that fill the average paleo cookbooks, and indulge yourself in savory Saffron Cauli-rice, the minty goodness of Celery Bison Stew, and gorgeous blood red Beet Noodles.

This book has something for everyone, from GAPS beginners who will appreciate a basic Meat Stock recipe to advanced chefs and GAPSters who will want to know details about Organ Meat Hot Pockets.

Dessert has not been forgotten! The Pumpkin Bars recipe is absolute heaven.

Look closely, as Nakisa has thoughtfully labelled each recipe for which kind of healthy diet it aligns with. This book is not strictly GAPS, but includes SCD (specific carbohydrate diet), paleo, WAP (Weston A Price Foundation), ketogenic, and low-FODMAPs (for SIBO sufferers) recipes as well.

If you are one of the increasing number of people emphasizing ancestral, nutrient-dense foods, and are curious about GAPS, this book will offer you variety from your usual fare and is a great place to start to see the GAPS diet in action.

And for those who having been eating a GAPS Diet for a long time and are ready to transition off, Nakisa's book is one of the few that includes some of those transitional recipes.

So jump in to a book filled with turmeric and saffron, of goose and lamb, of cauliflower and pumpkin. I hope you are as inspired as I am, and I wish you and your families the very best of health!

Liz

Liz Voosen, NTP, CGP, FDN-P

CHAPTER ONE: Why Writing This Book?

CHAPTER TWO: What is Gut and Psychology Syndrome Nutritional Diet (GAPS)

CHAPTER THREE: Recipes

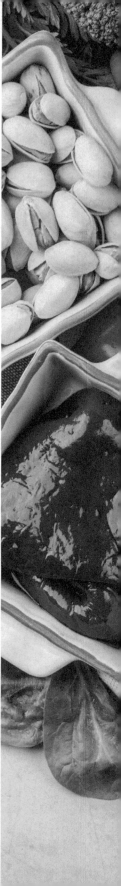

Breakfast

Lunch

Appetizer: Side Dish

Broth and Soups

Salads

Dinner

Snack Food

Dessert

CHAPTER ONE

Why Writing
This Book?

I have always been interested in health and nutrition. During my teenage years, I was always on various diets because I always had to watch what I ate because of always being on the heavy side. When I was in elementary school, my classmates used to call me bademjun koochooloo (little eggplant), because I was short and stubby. So I started dieting to erase that label. I would do prolonged fasting and try various diets and any new fad diet that came about to lose the extra weight. Boy, wasn't I able to lose it so fast? But I would gain it back right away and more so of it. When I turned 18, I decided I had enough of this constant dieting. After losing my extra weight, I started exercising and watching my weight very closely like a hawk. As soon as it slightly went up, I would get it back down with dieting and more rigorous exercising. I was finally able to overcome my weight struggles with this new tactic. Fast forward, when I came to the USA in my mid 20s, I would spend hours in grocery stores reading the packaged food labels and ingredients trying to make sense of them. I could not even pronounce over 50% of the ingredients on the list, but I thought it could be because I was not raised in America, so I started asking my native friends for help but no one knew

either. Originally, I was overwhelmed with the many brand varieties of the same packaged food, like there was a whole isle of breakfast cereal boxes, so many to choose from! But as I started reading the ingredients of these varieties, I soon learned how little choices there actually were in the market and how little nutrients they all had. I was surprised how much chemicals, preservatives, food colors, and flavor enhancers were added in those packaged food to increase their shelf life and to make them more attractive to the consumers and more profitable for the manufacturers. Everything had added sugar in it regardless of being a sweet or savory food. Two of the main ingredients I found in almost all packaged food were corn and soy. I was puzzled why over 42% of American adults and nearly 20% of children were obese when there were all these low calorie diet food and drinks and all these weight loss drugs and programs. According to Center for Disease Control, in the United States, the percentage of obese people, increased more than three times since the 1970s.

www.cdc.gov

60% of American adults and 27% of children have a chronic disease and the prevalence of it is alarmingly on the rise.

www.cdc.gov

When I was a child, my grandfather once burnt one single Cheetos and it burnt like a piece of plastic. He was trying to explain to us how bad that snack was for our body. He told us he never had snacks growing up. He would only eat "real" healthy food in small amounts. My grandfather, who lived to be almost 100 years old, didn't know anything about any of the fad diets of my time: the low calorie, low fat, high protein, high fat, vegan, vegetarian, pescetarian, etc. He did not know anything about protein shakes where you drink your food rather than chewing your food. He didn't have access to proper medical care, so when he got

sick, he used home remedies that he had learned from his mother who had in turn learned it from her own mother passed on to her generations after generations. When I came to the US, I was surprised how physicians in my family were recommending Tylenol like candies for every little headache or any other discomfort.

When my first son was born, I became even more careful in what I was feeding my family. With the birth of my second son and his birth injuries, I started to search for alternative medicine and nutritional/life style support to reduce the inflammation in his body and to help his body heal itself from the trauma of birth. I am pleased to say that both my boys are doing beautifully and making me proud every day. I wrote this book to pass on the recipes I created to successfully move though stages of GAPS Nutritional Protocol which is a very effective anti-inflammatory diet. I also included recipes to accomodate other anti-inflammatory diets. I hope you find this book helpful and enjoy making these nutrient-dense recipes for your family.

CHAPTER TWO

What is Gut and Psychology Syndrome Nutritional Diet (GAPS)

Dr. Natasha Campbell McBride, a neurosurgeon and nutritionist in England developed the GAPS nutritional protocol in 1998. GAPS is a gut-healing anti-inflammatory protocol and it stands for Gut and Psychology Syndrome and it evolved from Specific Carbohydrate Diet. Dr. Natasha believes that all diseases start in the gut, and by healing the gut, digestive, neurological, autoimmune disorders and many more health issues will be alleviated.

GAPS is a powerful anti-inflammatory nutritional protocol for addressing leaky gut issues. Leaky guts or intestinal permeability condition has been discussed in the medical literature for over 100 years. The intestinal epithelium houses gut microbiota, millions of microbes living in a symbiotic relationship with each other and with the human body. Intestinal epithelial cells have tight junctions and form a strong barrier separating the body from outside world. When these tight junctions and the balance of gut microbiota are compromised, they will channel the passage of toxins in the lumen of intestine to enter the blood stream creating havoc in the body and increasing the chance of developing chronic and autoimmune disorders.

www.nih.gov

In the year 2015, my family and I started GAPS nutritional protocol aiming to fix our leaky guts and to reduce my children's asthma/allergy symptoms, frequent eczema, and constant complaint of joint pain and tummy aches. After two intense years on this nutritional protocol, all the mentioned symptoms were diminished. Before we started GAPS, I asked our asthma/allergist about it. He discouraged me saying that it's a waste of time and money, as diet has nothing to do with asthma. The boys allergy symptoms have reduced but not completely gone; however, their asthma is completely non-existence. I used to have to fill their costly Asthma prescription on a monthly basis.

www.amazon.com

What Foods are Eliminated on the GAPS Diet?

All inflammatory foods such as grains, starches, processed sugar, artificial food colorings/additives, preservatives, refined vegetable oils and any processed/packaged foods are eliminated.

What Foods are Allowed on the GAPS Diet?

Homemade meat stock, non-starchy vegetables, grass-fed meat and wild fish/seafood, lots of healthy animal fats, organ meats, fermented dairy and fermented vegetables are the core principles of the diet. Raw unfiltered honey and dried fruits can be used in small amounts as sweeteners.
Dr. Natasha recommends organic non-GMO fruits and vegetables and organic 100% grass-fed meat whenever possible, but it is not critical if it is either too difficult to find or too pricey for the family's budget.

What Stages are there to the GAPS Diet?

There are three parts to GAPS Diet: the Introduction Diet ,the Full GAPS Diet, and Coming off the GAPS Diet.

The Introduction Diet has six stages and takes about 6 weeks to complete; however, it might take much longer depending on the person's state of health. The GAPS Diet takes two years or more depending on the condition(s) being treated. Coming off the GAPS Diet should be gradual, introducing new foods every 3-5 days. Under no condition, the patient should ever go back to the Standard American Diet (SAD).

Where Do I Start?

People with severe digestive issues should start with the Introduction Diet. Otherwise, the Full GAPS Diet is a good start for most others; especially if one is overwhelmed by the diet and the amount of work involved.

Recommended Supplements on the GAPS Diet

For the first 6 months on the diet, Dr Natasha recommends taking a good strength probiotics such as Bio-Kult brand

www.amazon.com

www.amazon.com

A good cod liver oil such as Nordic Naturals brand,

vitamin and mineral supplements such as Thorne Basic Nutrients

www.amazon.com

www.amazon.com

and if needed digestive enzymes such as Panplex 2-phase by Integrative Therapeutics

and Concentrace Mineral Drop from TraceMinerals

www.amazon.com

GAPS Lifestyle

It's important to note that the GAPS nutritional protocol is not only a diet, but a way of life. While we change our diet and heal our guts, there are additional things we can do to support our bodies. Therefore, we recommend some of the following lifestyle changes as well.

- For a gentle detoxification, Epsom-salt baths three times a week and daily vegetable juicing are recommended by Dr Natasha.

- To reduce the general toxic load, household cleaning agents and personal care products should be checked carefully. Only truly natural products are allowed. A good source to find clean natural products is "wellnessmama.com" and Dr. Natasha's website.

- Indoor plants such as Aloe Vera are recommended in the house to reduce the air toxic load.

- We developed a "no shoe" policy inside the house, as this is a major culprit in bringing in outside toxins indoor. We also air the inside of the house everyday by leaving all windows open during the day. People don't realize that indoor air quality is much worse than outdoor air quality! A good air purifier such as Honeywell is a great addition to any house.

- To reduce the toxic load, do not buy new furniture while on GAPS diet and do not remodel your house.

- To reduce the toxicity of the electromagnetic field radiation, we replaced our cordless phone with a corded one, turned off the Wi-Fi box at night, and used Ethernet hard wires when possible during the day. We also changed all of our energy-efficient light bulbs with the traditional LED ones. There is a lot more that can be done to protect yourself from the dangerous effects of EMF radiation. For more information on this subject, please visit ww.theelectricsense.com.

Can You be a Vegetarian on GAPS? How Do You Deal With Food Cravings?

GAPS recommends a list of food that can be tailored to each individual's taste and preference. A vegetarian individual can easily do GAPS diet. I, myself, prefer a vegetarian diet to meat diet and I was able to successfully stay on the GAPS Diet for almost two years. So, the GAPS Diet is not necessarily a high protein, a high fat, or low carbohydrate diet. Dr. Natasha believes that a person's body will dictate which food to consume on a daily basis and at a given time, so there is no limit in the amount of food to eat and the individual is free to choose among GAPS-allowed items for whatever their body craves to eat on each day. For example, one can choose to eat salad every day for as long as he/she wishes for.

Who Will Benefit From the GAPS Diet?

Anyone with inflammation in their body, anyone with digestive, autoimmune, and neurological disorders will benefit from the GAPS Diet along with those who have weight issues, asthma/allergies, diabetes, thyroid disorders and skin disorders (e.g., eczema, acne). However, keep in mind that GAPS is only a piece of the puzzle in solving the chronic disorders and is not the answer to everything. It's a good starting point, but you do need many other interventions to get full recovery.

How Do You Do GAPS on a Budget?

While Dr. Natasha recommends organic food whenever possible, this is not an absolute "must". If you are struggling with finances, buy your groceries from wherever your budget allows. You will still benefit from the healing power of GAPS Diet that way. Alternatively, Farmer's Markets are great places to find non-certified organic fruits and vegetables at cheaper prices with higher nutrient contents. We usually rotate among our farmers to ensure we get a variety of nutrients based on the animal feed and the health of the soil. Trader Joe's and Sprouts are also great stores for clean foods at reasonable prices. ThriveMarket.com sells a lot of the same foods as Mother's, Sprouts and Whole Foods online at a fraction of the price. Vitacost.com is a good place to buy your nutritional supplements at a discounted price.

How We Started Our GAPS Journey

Before we started on the GAPS Diet, I decided that we were going to start on a particular day. We started ours on Valentine's Day 2015 in the name of love. Even though the end date of GAPS Diet is very individualized depending on the person and his/her state of health, I also decided to give my family an end date. Dr. Natasha recommends staying on the diet for at least one and half year to two years after the start of Full GAPS diet. Our finish date was set two years from the start of the Introductory GAPS Diet. I figured that even if we had to continue GAPS beyond that point, we could continue keeping our home GAPS-legal while allowing the kids to participate in social aspect of eating with friends so they did not feel left out.

The day before starting the diet, we cleaned out our cupboards and the entire house from any un-allowed GAPS items. Our refrigerator was almost completely empty when we were done. There was some meat and some vegetables and that's all. A week before starting the GAPS Diet and throughout the time we were on the diet, we visualized succeeding and achieving our goal, which was improv-ing or alleviating the children's asthma symptoms and reducing their food allergies.

How We Overcame Obstacles

There were times when we thought that we couldn't possibly continue. There were many times when my family got tired of it and I was exhausted from having to cook and clean constantly. Although Dr. Natasha discourages eating out during the first stages of the diet, I would say take a quick break if you need to! It is okay to go out for a meal even when you are at the beginning stages. Just remember which stage you are on your GAPS journey. Only order the allowed items. To be on the safe side, ask the server for grilled meat and steamed vegetables without any sauce and any vegetable oil.

How to Succeed on the GAPS Diet

Visualization techniques are a powerful tool at your disposal for not giving up. Visualize the finish line when you have reached your goal. Talk about the foods you miss and your cravings. We would talk about how much we missed chocolate croissants, but then we would remind ourselves that we can have it after we are done with the diet. That's why I decided to set a finish date for us; so we had a goal we could mark and see on a calendar.

How to Come off the GAPS Diet

When you feel you are healed and ready to come off the GAPS Diet, it is recommended to start introducing un-allowed items one at a time and then wait 3-5 days, before introducing something new. Do not introduce more than one item at a time. Wheat and other gluten should be the last items to be introduced. We introduced Einkorn wheat

www.amazon.com

first for a few months before introducing modern wheat. In both cases, sprouted grains are soaked overnight in filtered water containing one tablespoon of whey or plain yogurt to facilitated the digestion of gluten.

An inexpensive reasonable whole-house water system can be purchased from Radiant Life

https://radiantlifecatalog.com

It's carbon filter and removes floride, chlorine and chloramine, and VOCs).

How Does the GAPS Diet Compare to Ketogenic, Paleolithic, SIBO, and Weston A Price Foundation Dietary Recommendations?

These anti-inflammatory diets are similar in many aspects and different in others. Let's take a quick look at them. In general, all three diets promote eating real food and recommend grass-fed meat, wild caught fish/seafood, eggs, fresh vegetables, nuts and seeds, and healthy fat. All inflammatory foods are eliminated; so no grains, no gluten, no soy, and no processed foods are allowed.

Gut and Psycology Syndrome Nutritional Diet (GAPS)

GAPS is more of a lifestyle change than just a diet as it includes a detox and a nutritional supplement components as well. The staple foods in GAPS include lots of healthy animal fat, homemade meat stock and fermented dairy/vegetables. No corn and no soy are allowed.

https://www.gapsdiet.com

Ketogenic Diet (KETO)

Keto diet is a high fat, moderate protein, very low carbohydrates diets and lots of leafy vegetables but no starchy vegetables are allowed. No Legumes nor grains are allowed. The idea behind keto diet is to empty out the carbohydrate reserves in the body to start burning fat. Basically, you will be in ketosis state meaning you will use fats as your fuel resources. A clean Keto diet uses pure stevia or monk fruit as a sweetener, but many keto dieters use alcohol sugar which is very harsh on the digestive system and not allowed on GAPS diet.

www.healthline.com

Paleolithic Diet (PALEO)

Paleo, or the caveman diet, is our ancestral diet. It's more restrictive than GAPS and WAPF diets but less restrictive than Ketogenic diet. Some oils such as coconut, flax seed, olive, macadamia, avocado, and walnut are allowed. No dairy, no grains, and no legumes are allowed.

www.mayoclinic.org

Small Intestinal Bacterial Overgrowth Diet (SIBO) – Low FODMAP

SIBO is a digestive disorder characterized by excessive bacterial overgrowth in the small intestine which then ferment to cause bloating diarrhea, and other digestive symptoms. To treat SIBO, Low FODMAP diet is usually prescribed. FODMAP refers to certain fermentable sugars known to trigger digestive problem.

www.dietvsdisease.org

Weston-A-Price- Foundation- Whole-Food Nature-Based Diet (WAPF)

The WAPF Diet is based on the findings of Cleveland dentist Weston A Price. WAPF nutrient-dense, unprocessed diet promotes locally-sourced special foods like cod liver oil, fish, raw eggs, organ meats, animal fat, raw cream and butter, and raw unpasteurized whole milk from grass-fed cows.

Traditional lacto-fermented foods and soft drinks, homemade bone broths, Properly prepared whole grains (soaked overnight), traditional sourdough breads, and unrefined salt are among WAPF recommendations. WAPF dieters avoid vegetable oils, margarine, GMO soy and corn, and low fat diet. My family and I follow WAPF diet.

CHAPTER THREE

Recipes

Breakfast

Cashew Pancake

GAPS, KETO, PALEO, SIBO, WAPF

Ingredients

- 1 cup raw cashews
- 1 cup water
- 1 tablespoon melted goat ghee
- 1 teaspoon baking soda
- 1 teaspoon ground cinnamon
- A pinch of sea salt
- 4 large eggs
- 2 teaspoons pure vanilla extract

Instructions

- Combine cashews and water in a blender and blend until completely mealed.
- Add the rest of the ingredients and blend for 2 more min.
- Make the pancakes in a pancake frying pan on medium low, 5 min on each side, cover and flip for another 5 min when edges start to brown and you see bubbles coming out the sides.

Milkshake

GAPS, KETO, PALEO, SIBO, WAPF

Ingredients

- 1 Carrot
- 1 apple or pear
- 1 stick of celery
- 1 small yellow beet
- 2 organic raw duck eggs
- 4 tablespoons of raw homemade cream fraiche
- 1 tablespoon Organic Pasture X-factor butter
  http://www.greenpasture.org/product/concentrated-butter-oil-liquid/
- 2 teaspoon Nordic Naturals cod liver oil
  https://www.nordicnaturals.com/consumers/arctic-cod-liver-oil

Instructions

🍽 Juice the vegetables in a juicer. Add the rest of the ingredients in a blender and blend the mixture together.

Tuna Omelets
GAPS, KETO, PALEO, SIBO, WAPF

Ingredients

- 3 tablespoon ghee
- 6 scrambled eggs
- 1 can tuna drained from the brine and dried on paper towel
- 1 tablespoon chopped green pepper
- ½ cup chopped tomatoes
- 1 pk of 8 oz organic shredded mozzarella

Instructions

- Preheat oven to 350 degrees.
- Melt the ghee in an oven safe baking dish by placing the dish inside the heated oven for 5 min
- Add the eggs, tuna, green bell pepper and tomatoes, salt and pepper to taste, cover with cheese.
- Bake for 30 minutes.

Lunch

Cheesy Chile

GAPS, KETO, PALEO, SIBO, WAPF

Ingredients

- 4 Anaheim chile peppers, charred and peeled
- 4 tablespoon mozzarella cheese, grated
- 4 tablespoons coconut oil
- Salt and pepper to taste

Instructions

- ◉ Remove seeds and skin from peppers. Stuff each pepper with one tablespoon grated cheese.
- ◉ Pour the oil in a frying pan and heat over medium-high heat.
- ◉ Fry until lightly browned on both sides. Serve with some fried mushrooms.

Leafy Vegetable Crustless Quiche

GAPS, KETO, PALEO, SIBO, WAPF

Ingredients

- ½ cup green onion
- ½ cup parsley
- ½ cup dill
- ¼ cup basil
- 1 cup spinach leaves
- ¼ cup fresh fenugreek leaves
- ¼ cup mint leaves
- ¼ cup dandelions
- 5 eggs
- 2 teaspoons ground turmeric
- Salt and pepper to taste
- ½ cup coconut oil

Instructions

- Use a food processor to finely chop all the greens.Transfer to a mixing bowl.
- Whisk eggs, turmeric, salt and pepper into the mixed greens until fully incorporated.
- Heat the coconut oil in a non-stick green pan at medium-low heat.
- Add the mixture to the pan and quickly spread it into an even layer.
- Cover and cook for about 15 min, until the bottom is browned and the eggs are set and the mixture is not runny any more.
- With the side of a wooden spatula divide the large pancake into quarters and with the help of a silicon spatula, flip over each quarter while holding the top of each each quarter with the wooden spatula.
- Continue cooking the flipped side until the bottom is browned, about 10min.
- Cut each quarter in half to make 8 slices.
- Serve with grain-free flat bread.

Mushroom Cauli-Rissoto

GAPS, KETO, PALEO, SIBO, WAPF

Ingredients

- 1 large head cauliflower, cut into florets, riced
- 2 tablespoons ghee
- 1 tablespoon fried onion
- ½ tablespoon fried garlic
- 1 cup shiitake mushrooms, thinly sliced
- 1 cup shredded mozzarella cheese
- ½ cup parmesan cheese
- 1 tablespoon Fresh parsley, chopped
- ¼ teaspoon saffron
- Salt and pepper, to taste

Instructions

- Sauté the mushrooms in ghee for about 5-7 min. Add the fried onion and garlic and stir for another 5 min.
- Add the cauli-rice, saffron, and Mozzarella and Parmesan cheese and cook for about 5 min, stirring occasionally.
- Add salt and pepper to taste. Garnish with chopped fresh parsley.

Potato Crustless Quiche
WAPF

Ingredients

- 6 medium potatoes, grated
- 7 large eggs
- Salt and pepper to taste
- 1 teaspoons turmeric
- 5 tablespoons extra virgin coconut oil for frying

Instructions

- Add all ingredients and mix well.
- Heat the coconut oil in a large pan over medium heat. pour the mixture in the pan and cover with a lid.
- Once you see that the bottom has turned a golden brown and the top has set and is no longer watery, cut the pancake in quarters and flip each quarter over and let it cook for another 15-20min under low medium heat.
- To flip the quarters successfully, use two spatula one underneath and one over the piece.

Spinach Kale Quiche
GAPS, KETO, PALEO, SIBO, WAPF

Ingredients

- 1 (9 inch) frozen pie crust
- 4 tablespoon ghee
- 1 tablespoon fried shallot
- 1 tablespoon fried garlic
- 2 cup finely chopped spinach
- 2 cups finely chopped baby kale
- 1 cup finely chopped crimini mushrooms
- 3 duck eggs
- ⅔ cup grated Parmesan cheese
- ½ cup grated mozzarella cheese
- ¾ cup sour cream
- Salt and pepper to taste

Instructions

- Preheat oven to 350 Farenheit degrees.
- Bake the pie crust for 10 minutes in the oven and remove just before it turns brown.
- Mix all the ingredients except cheese and sour cream and cook in ghee for 10minutes.
- Add the sour cream and cheese and mix well.
- Pour mixture into the pie crust.
- Bake in the oven for 30 minutes.

Turkey Potato Patties
WAPF

Ingredients

- 1 lb ground turkey
- 2 large potatoes, baked and grated
- 1 medium onion, grated
- 1 teaspoon turmeric
- 1 egg
- 3-5 tablespoon duck fat
- Salt and pepper to taste

Instructions

- Mix all the ingredients very well (except for the duck fat)
- In a large pan, heat the duck fat, make small patties with the mixture and place them one by one in the pan.
- Flip the patties over after one side turns golden brown.

Appetizer
Side Dish

Basic Cooked Rice

SIBO, WAPF

Ingredients

- 2 cups sprouted basmati rice
- 6 cups filtered water
- 2 tablespoons coconut oil
- 2 tablespoons salt

Instructions

- In a pot, pre-soak the white rice overnight in 3 cups of filtered water and one tablespoon whey or plain yogurt to facilitate the digestion of this grain.

- The next day, rinse the rice with tap water several times until the water that covers the rice is clear.

- Drain the water out. Add 3 cups of filtered water to the rice.

- Add the salt and coconut oil.

- Bring to a boil. Reduce the heat to low and let cook covered for 30 minutes.

Beets Noodle
GAPS, KETO, PALEO, SIBO, WAPF

Ingredients

- 2-3 tablespoon of butter
- 5 medium sized red beets, skinned
- ½ cup chopped shitaki mushroom
- ¼ cup chopped white radish
- 1 tablespoon fresh parsley, finely chopped
- 1 teaspoon of crushed garlic
- 1 tablespoon of fried onion
- Salt and pepper to taste

Instructions

- Place each beet in your Spiralizer and make spiral beet noodles.
- Fry the mushrooms in butter until they start to soften (about 10 minutes). Add garlic, fried onion, and chopped parsley and radishes and stir for another 5 min in medium heat.
- Cook the beet noodles along with all the other ingredients over the medium heat for 8-10 minutes until soft, stirring them around occasionally.
- Mix the mushrooms with beet noodles

Blended Duck Liver

GAPS, KETO, PALEO, SIBO, WAPF

Ingredients

- 5 lb duck liver, all fat removed

Instructions

- 🍽 Blend in the duck liver in a blender.
- 🍽 Until a smooth watery paste is formed.
- 🍽 Pour the blended liver into 1 ounce ice cube trays with lid and store in the freezer until ready to use in recipes.

Fried Onion, Shallot, or Garlic

GAPS, KETO, PALEO, SIBO, WAPF

Ingredients

- 5 large yellow onions/10 shallots or 10 garlic, chopped
- 3 tablespoons lard or tallow https://fatworks.com/collections/Single-Jar
- 1 tablespoon turmeric

Instructions

- Heat the oil in a large pan on high for two minutes
- Add the chopped onion with turmeric and lower the heat to medium-low
- Stir until the onion is caramelized and browned (about 15-20minutes).
- Wait until the onion cools down to room temperature
- Using 4oz glass mason jars,
- Spoon 1-2 tablespoons of the fried onion in each jar and store in the freezer for future use in recipes.
- When ready to use, thaw the fried onion in the refrigerator a day prior to using it in your recipes.

Fried Vegetables

GAPS, KETO, PALEO, SIBO, WAPF

Ingredients

- 2 cups chopped swiss chard
- ½ cup chopped red pepper
- 1 cup chopped yellow zucchini
- ½ cup chopped sugar snaps
- Salt and pepper to taste
- 2-3 tablespoon lard

Instructions

- Mix the meatball ingredients well in a bowl
- Make small meatballs. If the mixture is runny, use a round spoon and drop a small mass, the size of a meatball on the pan
- Fry them in 1 tablespoon lard for 5 min each side
- Fry the chopped greens and vegetables for 10 min in 2-3 tablespoons lard and add salt and pepper.
- Serve the meatballs on top of fried vegetables

Mushroom with Carrot Leaves

GAPS, KETO, PALEO, SIBO, WAPF

Ingredients

- 1 cup equal amount of oyster, enoki, and shitaki mushrooms, chopped
- ¼ cup chopped carrot leaves
- ½ teaspoon turmeric
- 1 tablespoon fried onion
- 4 tablespoon coconut oil
- salt and pepper to taste

Instructions

- Fry the chopped carrot leaves in oil until the color changes to dark green. Add the fried onion and chopped mushrooms and continue frying the mushrooms for another 10min. Serve as a side dish with BBQ meat.

Purple Sweet Potato with Red Cabbage

SIBO, WAPF

Ingredients

- 1 purple sweet potatoes
- ½ cup chopped red cabbage
- 1 tablespoon fried onion
- 1 tablespoon ghee
- Salt and pepper to taste
- 1 tablespoon shredded mozzarella cheese

Instructions

- Bake the potatoes in the oven at 400F for 45 min. Cut the potatoes lengthwise after baked.
- While the potatoes are being baked, stir fry the chopped red cabbage in ghee for 10min until soft and add the fried onion. Salt and pepper to taste.
- Stuff the potato with the red cabbage filling and garnish with mozzarella cheese.

Red Cabbage Rice

SIBO, WAPF

Ingredients

- 1 cup cooked rice
- ½ cup shredded red cabbage
- 3 tablespoon ghee
- 1 tablespoon fried onion
- ¼ cup cut celery
- ⅛ cup chopped red pepper
- Salt and pepper to taste

Instructions

- Sauté red cabbage in the ghee, then add the fried onion, celery, and red pepper. Cook for 15-20 minutes on medium-low heat.
- Add salt and pepper to taste.
- Stir and let cook for 15 minutes under medium low heat.
- Mix this into the cooked rice in a large pot, cover, and let cook for 15 minutes

Saffron Cauli-Rice

GAPS, KETO, PALEO, SIBO, WAPF

Ingredients

- 1 medium size cauliflower, chopped to small florets
- ½ cup berberries
- ¼ cup honey
- 3 tablespoons ghee
- Salt and pepper to taste

Instructions

- Process the cauliflower florets in a processor until it looks like rice grains.
- Add 3 tablespoons ghee on a large saucepan, add the cauli-rice and salt, cover and cook for 20 minutes.
- Sauté the barberries in honey and ghee for 10 min until translucent.
- Put the cauli-rice on a serving plate and decorate the top with saffron and sautéed barberries.
- In transition GAPS, 2 cups of cooked can replace the cauli-rice.

Sauerkraut
GAPS, KETO, PALEO, SIBO, WAPF

Ingredients

- 1 large organic cabbage head
- 2 tablespoons Himalayan sea salt

Instructions

- Cut the cabbage into quarters, cut out the core and put in your compost pile,
- Thinly slice the cabbage.
- Add the salt, using both hands, massage the cabbage mixture for 10min until it produces salt brine liquid.
- Transfer the mixture and its liquid to a 6-quart mason jar, Pack the cabbage down with you fist. Make sure the cabbage is completely covered in liquid. If not, add enough additional salt brine mixture to cover the cabbage.
- Place a bag full of salt brine as a weight on top of the cabbage mixture and leave the jar at room temperature for 10 days before transferring it into the refrigerator for up to 6 months.

Broth and Soups

Butternut Squash Soup
GAPS, KETO, PALEO, SIBO, WAPF

Ingredients

- 1 medium-size butternut squash
- 1 tablespoon fried onion (see recipe)
- 1 tablespoon fried garlic (see recipe)
- 5 cups homemade chicken broth (see recipe)
- 4 tablespoons chicken paste (see recipe)
- ½ teaspoon cloves
- ½ teaspoon chipotle chili
- ¼ teaspoon black pepper
- 1 teaspoon dried fennel
- Salt to taste
- ½ cup homemade raw crème fraiche (see recipe)

Instructions

- In a pre-heated oven, bake the whole butternut squash for 1h at 400F.
- After the squash cooled down, cut the squash in half lengthwise, take the flesh out and save. Discard the skin and seeds.
- In a Breville food processor, add the squash and the rest of the ingredients and process until smooth.
- Pour the mixture in a pot and heat until boil.
- Remove from heat and add the crème fraiche and serve.

Chicken Wing Soup
GAPS, KETO, PALEO, SIBO, WAPF

Ingredients

- 1 lb chicken wing
- 1 kohlrabi bulb, peeled, cut to tiny pieces
- 1 cup mushrooms
- 1 small purple cauliflower
- 5 medium size Carrots
- 2 green zucchini
- 10 yellow baby squash, cut in half
- 1 large onion, cut to small pieces
- ½ cup cherry tomatoes
- 3 tablespoons lime juice
- 2 teaspoons saffron
- Salt and pepper

Instructions

- Rinse the chicken wings and put them in the crockpot and cover with filtered water.
- Coarsely process all vegetables, except the cherry tomatoes, in the Breville food processor using the chopping blade.
- Add the processed vegetables and cherry tomatoes to the crockpot and add more water to cover the vegetables.
- Add the saffron, lime juice, salt and pepper.
- Let it cook for 10hrs.

Chicken Heart and Gizzard Soup

GAPS, KETO, PALEO, SIBO, WAPF

Ingredients

- 1 lb chicken heart (cleaned and fat removed)
- 1 lb chicken gizzard (cleaned with inner skin peeled off)
- 1 large onion, diced
- 2 cloves garlic, diced
- 1 celery stalk, diced
- 1 red bell pepper, diced
- 3 carrots, diced
- 5 cups homemade chicken bone broth (see recipe)
- 4 tablespoons chicken paste (see recipe)
- 2 large tomatoes, diced
- 1 pack of sliced fresh mushroom
- 2 tablespoons chopped parsley
- 2 teaspoons turmeric
- Salt and pepper to taste

Instructions

- Add all ingredients in your Crockpot and cook on low heat for 10 hours.

Chicken Bone Broth
GAPS, KETO, PALEO, SIBO, WAPF

Ingredients

- 5 lb chicken feet
- 5 lb chicken head
- 1 large onion, diced
- 1 clove garlic, crushed
- 1 tablespoon turmeric

Instructions

- Put all ingredients in the crockpot and cover with filtered water until all meat are submerged.
- Cook on low heat for 7 hours.
- Pass the broth through a sieve into a pot and save the feet and head.
- Concentrate by heating the broth on medium heat until the liquid has reduced to half.
- You can also heat reduce the bone broth to $\frac{1}{10}$ of the original liquid amount and freeze the concentrated broth in 16oz mason jars for future use (2 cups/jar).
- When ready, thaw the concentrated broth in the refrigerator overnight; add 3 cups filtered water and use in recipes. It makes a total of 5 cups.

Chicken Paste and Chicken Bone Broth

- Pull apart the meat and skin from cooked feet and head and save the bones. Make sure there is no bone left in the meat/skin mixture by examining the mixture with your hands.

- Blend the mixture with a hand-held blender until becomes like a paste

- Pour 4 tablespoons of the paste in 4oz mason jars and freeze.

- When ready to use, thaw the paste overnight in the refrigerator and add to your soup recipes.

- Put the saved bones from step 7 back in the crockpot.

- Pour enough filtered water to cover the bones.

- Add 1 tablespoon apple cider vinegar Cook in low heat for 24 hours.

- Sieve and throw away the bones.

- Concentrate the bone broth as in step 4 and store in the freezer for future use.

Chicken Stock Recipe

GAPS, KETO, PALEO, SIBO, WAPF

Ingredients

- 5 lb chicken thigh or beef oxtail
- 1 large onion, diced
- 1 carrot, chopped
- 1 celery stick, chopped
- 1 teaspoon peppercorn
- 1 tablespoon salt
- ½ tablespoon dried rosemary

Instructions

- In a crockpot, add all the ingredients and cover with enough water that all the meat is submerged.
- Cook on low for 24-48 hours.
- Sieve the meat stock in a pot and save the meat to use in soups or stews.
- Reduce the liquid to half by heating on the stove on medium heat.
- Let it cool before pouring into 8oz jars for freezing.
- When ready to use, thaw the meat stock overnight in the refrigerator.

Fish Bone Broth
GAPS, KETO, PALEO, SIBO, WAPF

Ingredients

- 5 lb wild salmon bones and head
- Salt and pepper to taste
- 1 tablespoon crushed garlic

Instructions

- Place the bones and head and tail inside a stockpot and cover with filtered water.
- Add the turmeric, salt, and pepper
- Cook on medium high for 30 min.
- Sieve the broth and store in the freezer in divided batches.
- On the bones, tail, and head, separate the fish meat from the bones and head and add to your soup

High-Gelatin Nutritious Soup
GAPS, KETO, PALEO, SIBO, WAPF

Ingredients

- 2 pig feet
- 1 lb chicken feet (cut nails and throw away)
- 1 lb chicken head
- 1 lb beef feet
- 2 cross cut beef bone marrow
- 1 onion, chopped
- 4 carrots, chopped
- 4 stalks of celery, chopped
- 1 tablespoon crushed garlic
- 1 tablespoon dried rosemary
- 1 teaspoon dried thyme
- 1 tablespoon turmeric
- 1 tablespoon salt
- 2 teaspoon pepper
- ½ teaspoon crushed hot chili pepper
- 2 tablespoon vinegar
- ½ cup chopped mint
- ½ cup chopped parsley
- 1 tablespoon lard or tallow
- Filtered water, enough to cover the bones

Instructions

- Put all the ingredients (from the pig feet to crushed hot chili pepper) in a crockpot

- Let cook for 10 hours on low.

- Strain the soup through a stainless steel sieve and leave the broth at room temperature to cool down before storing it in the fridge.

- When cooled down to room temperature, pull off the meat, ligaments and skin from the feet and head, and scoop out the bone marrow from the bone. Save in the refrigerator.

- Save all the leftover bones and put them back in the crockpot along with 2 tablespoons vinegar and cover with filtered water. Let it cook for 24 hours on low to get the minerals out of bones.

Strain the broth and combine this second run of bone broth with the first batch.

- Using a blender, gently blend the pulled off meat, ligaments and marrow along with the cooked vegetables. Add 1 tablespoon turmeric.

- Fry the mint and parsley in lard or tallow until darkens color.

- In a pot, combine the bone broth, blended ligaments and meat, and fried herbs. Heat the pot on high until the soup boils, then lower the heat to medium and let simmer for 30 minutes before serving.

Lamb Neck Soup

GAPS, KETO, PALEO, SIBO, WAPF

Ingredients

- 5 lb lamb neck
- 1 large heirloom tomatoes grated
- 1 tablespoon fried onion (1 whole small onion, chopped and fried in 1 tablespoon lard)
- 1 tablespoon ghee
- 1 cup enoki mushroom
- ¼ cup chopped yellow carrots
- 1 cup cherry tomatoes
- ½ cup chopped baby bock Choy
- 1 teaspoon turmeric
- 1 fresh squeezed lemon
- Salt and pepper to taste

Instructions

- Place the lamb neck in a crockpot and cover with water. Cook for 10hr.
- Let it cool before separating the meat from bone. Use the meat in the soup.
- Put the bones back in the crockpot and cover it with water and 1 table-spoon vinegar. Cook for 24-36hr. Seive and add this broth to your soup later or save in the freezer for later use.
- In an oiled pan, add the onion and mushroom and fry on medium heat for 15 minutes until the mushroom is browned.
- Add the fried mushroom mix to the rest of the ingredients and cook in a covered pan on medium heat for 20 minutes.

Meat Stock
GAPS, KETO, PALEO, SIBO, WAPF

Ingredients

- 5 lb chicken neck or beef oxtail
- 1 large onion, diced
- 1 carrot, chopped
- 1 celery stick, chopped
- 1 teaspoon peppercorn
- 1 tablespoon salt
- ½ tablespoon dried rosemary

Instructions

- In a crockpot, add all the ingredients and cover with enough water that all the meat is submerged.
- Cook on low for 8-10 hours.
- Sieve the meat stock in a pot and save the meat to use in soups or stews.
- Reduce the liquid to half by heating on the stove on medium heat.
- Let it cool before pouring into 8oz jars for freezing.
- When ready to use, thaw the meat stock overnight in the refrigerator.

Seafood Soup
GAPS, KETO, PALEO, SIBO, WAPF

Ingredients

- 1 lb frozen seafood mixture (¼ lb of each shrimp, calamari, lobster, and scallop) leftover meat from fish bone broth (see recipe)
- ½ cup chopped arugula
- ½ cup chopped spinach
- ½ cup chopped bok choy
- ½ cup chopped fennel bulb
- 2 tablespoon avocado oil
- 1 teaspoon crushed garlic
- 1 teaspoon turmeric
- Salt and pepper to taste
- ⅛ teaspoon crushed chili
- 3-4 cups fish bone broth (see recipe) or filtered water

Instructions

- Thaw the frozen seafood gently in a colander under the running cold water for 5-6 min. Pat dry the seafood with paper towel.
- Sauté the chopped vegetables in oil for 5 min.
- Add the garlic, chili, turmeric, salt and pepper to the greens mixture.
- Add the seafood mixture and fish meat
- Add the fish broth and let it simmer for 5-6 minutes until the shrimp turns pink.

Salads

Olivieh Salad
WAPF

Ingredients

- 6 large eggs, hard boiled, chopped
- 6 medium boiled potatoes, chopped
- 1 medium carrots, peeled and steamed, chopped
- 1 cup frozen sweet peas, boiled for 15 min
- 10 baby dill pickles, chopped
- 1 ½ cups Primal Kitchen mayonnaise
- 1 tablespoon fresh lime juice
- Salt and pepper to taste

Instructions

- Add all the ingredients. add salt and pepper and mix well. Serve it in grain-free Baguette.

Pasta Duck Salad
GAPS, KETO, PALEO, SIBO, WAPF

Ingredients

- One 16 ounce package chickpeas rotini pasta
- 2 large duck breasts
- 1 cup chopped asparagus
- 1 cup chopped carrots
- 2 green onions sliced
- 1 cup Primal Kitchen mayonnaise
- 1 tablespoon fresh lemon juice
- 3 tablespoons olive oil
- salt and pepper to taste

Instructions

- Cook the pasta according to package directions, drain and rinse in cold water.
- Grill the duck breasts on your BBQ grill as desired and chop up into cubes. In a large bowl, place the cooked pasta, the duck and chopped vegetable.
- Add the lemon juice, olive oil, mayonnaise and add salt and pepper to taste.

Potato Salad
WAPF

Ingredients

- 2 large new/red potatoes
- 2 large avocados, sliced
- 2 atomic red carrots, chopped
- 1 teaspoon dried dill
- Salt and pepper to taste
- 2 tablespoons extra virgin olive oil
- 1 tablespoon freshly squeezed lime

Instructions

- Preheat oven to 350 degrees.
- Scrub the potatoes and use a fork to poke holes in it.
- Put directly in the oven on the center rack and bake for 45 minutes (it's done when you can easily stick a fork in it).
- Remove the potatoes from the oven and cool.
- Chop up the potatoes and mix the rest of the ingredients.
- Add salt and pepper to taste.

Red Cabbage Potato Coleslaw

GAPS, KETO, PALEO, SIBO, WAPF

Ingredients

- 1 tablespoon apple cider vinegar
- ¼ cup extra-virgin olive oil
- ½ cup chopped potato
- 1 small head red cabbage, thinly sliced
- 1 large yellow carrot, chopped
- ¼ cup pine nuts
- ⅓ cup raw walnuts, coarsely chopped
- ½ cup mayonnaise
- Salt and pepper to taste

Instructions

- Add all the ingredients together.
- Mix throughly with mayonnaise.

Dinner

Basic Oven-Baked Chicken Thigh
GAPS, KETO, PALEO, SIBO, WAPF

Ingredients

- 5 lb chicken thighs
- 5 tablespoon fried chopped onion (see recipes)
- 5 teaspoon turmeric
- 5 teaspoon salt
- 3 teaspoon pepper

Instructions

- Preheat oven at 350F.
- In a pyrex add the chicken thighs along with all the ingredients
- Cover with Aluminum foil and Leave in the oven for 2h

Butternut Squash Noodles with Roasted Goose

GAPS, KETO, PALEO, SIBO, WAPF

Ingredients

- 1 cup spiralized butternut squash
- 2 tablespoons olive oil
- ¼ cup cubed roasted goose breast
- ¼ cup chopped spinach
- ¼ cup chanterelles and wood ear mushrooms, chopped
- 1 tablespoon fresh parsley, finely chopped
- 1 teaspoon fresh mint, finely chopped
- ¼ cup fresh spinach, finely chopped
- 1 tablespoon fried onion
- 1 tablespoon goose fat
- 1 tablespoon olive oil
- Salt and pepper to taste

Instructions

- Preheat your oven to 350 degrees Fahrenheit.
- On an oven pan, toss the squash noodles with olive oil, salt & pepper.
- Spread them evenly on the pan and roast about 20 min until the edges just starting to brown.
- In the meantime, sauté the mushrooms in the goose fat for about 10min and add the fried onion, chopped herbs, and spinach and let it cook for another 5 min, stir occasionally.
- Remove the noodles from the oven and add the cubed goose breast and mushroom mixture to it and enjoy.

Cabbage Meatball

GAPS, KETO, PALEO, SIBO, WAPF

Ingredients

- 1 small red cabbage
- 3 tablespoon lard
- ½ cup chopped mushrooms
- 1 tablespoon fried onion
- Salt and pepper to taste
- 1 tablespoon turmeric
- 1 tablespoon turkey liver very finely chopped
- 1 lb ground dark turkey
- 1 teaspoon finely ground rosemary
- 1 teaspoon crushed garlic

Instructions

- Coarsely chop cabbage in a Breville food processor.
- Add lard in a pan, add the fried onion, mushrooms and shredded cabbage, salt/pepper, turmeric, cover and cook on low for 20-30 minutes. Make sure to stir occasionally.
- Grind the onion and remove the juice by squeezing it between two paper towels.
- Mix well the ground onion, meat, and salt/pepper, rosemary, and crushed garlic.
- Make little meatballs and cook in a greased covered pan in very low heat for 15 minutes or until browned.
- Gently mix the cabbage mix with the meatball, cook on low heat for 10 minutes and serve.

Celery Bison Stew

GAPS, KETO, PALEO, SIBO, WAPF

Ingredients

- 1 head celery, cut into 2 inch pieces
- 1 lb bison neck
- 1 bunch mint, minced
- 1 bunch parsley, minced
- 1 teaspoon turmeric
- 4 tablespoon bison tallow
- 1 tablespoon fried onion
- Salt and pepper to taste
- 1 tablespoon lime juice

Instructions

- Add the bison neck to the crockpot and cover with water and cook overnight until tender.
- Add turmeric, lime juice, salt and pepper to the crockpot.
- Fry the cut celery with 2 tablespoon tallow in a pan until they are slightly soft.
- Add the minced herbs to the celery pan, stir and fry along until the herbs become dark green.
- Add the herb/celery mixture to the bison crockpot and let it simmer for another hour before serving.

Chicken Cauli-Rice

GAPS, KETO, PALEO, SIBO, WAPF

Ingredients

- 1 medium size cauliflower, chopped to small florets
- 1 medium size baked potato, chopped into small pieces
- 1 red bell pepper, chopped
- ½ cup oven-baked chopped chicken thighs
- Salt and pepper to taste

Instructions

- Process the cauliflower florets in a Breville food processor from Amazon until it looks like rice grains.
- Add 3 tablespoons ghee on a large pan, add the cauliflower and salt cover and cook for 20 minutes. Stir occasionally.
- Mix the rest of the ingredients to the cauliflower and stir. Add salt and pepper to taste.
- Cook for another 10 minutes.

Chickpeas Pasta with Grilled Duck

PALEO, SIBO

Ingredients

- One 16 ounce package chickpeas rotini pasta
- 2 large duck breasts
- 1 cup chopped asparagus
- 1 cup chopped carrots
- 2 green onions sliced
- 1 cup mayonnaise
- 1 tablespoon fresh lemon juice
- 3 tablespoons olive oil
- Salt and pepper to taste

Instructions

- Cook the pasta according to package directions, drain and rinse in cold water.
- Grill the duck breasts on your BBQ grill as desired and chop up into cubes.
- In a large bowl, place the cooked pasta, the duck and chopped vegetable.
- Add the lemon juice, olive oil, and salt and pepper to taste.

Crustless Root Vegetable Quiche
GAPS, SIBO, WAPF

Ingredients

- 1 tablespoon olive oil
- ½ tablespoon fried shallot
- 1 cup chopped root vegetables (white radishes, turnip, parsnip)
- 2 large eggs
- ¼ cup milk
- ¼ cup grated mozzarella
- Salt and pepper to taste

Instructions

- Preheat the oven to 400°F.
- Spread the vegetables evenly in one layer in a 9x13in pyrex dish.
- Add the olive oil, fried shallot, salt, and pepper. Cover the dish with aluminum foil and bake for 40-45 min. Take it out of the oven and let cool down.
- In a bowl, mix the eggs, milk, and cheese and pour over the grilled vegetables.
- Transfer it back into the oven for 40-45 min until the top is slightly brown.

GAPS Organ Meatloaf
GAPS, KETO, PALEO, SIBO, WAPF

Ingredients

- ¼ lb turkey liver
- 1 lb Bison tongue
- ¼ lb turkey heart
- 1 yellow onion
- 3 cloves garlic
- ½ cup tomato paste
- 1 egg, whisked
- ¾ cup almond flour
- Salt and pepper, to taste

For the sauce

- 11 cup tomato paste
- ½ cup meat stock (see recipe)
- ½ teaspoon crushed garlic
- ½ cup fresh chopped parsley
- 1 tablespoon beef tallow
- 1 lime (squeezed)

- Salt and pepper, to taste
- ½ teaspoon crushed garlic
- ½ cup fresh chopped parsley
- 1 tablespoon beef tallow

Instructions

- Preheat oven to 350 degrees.
- In a meat grinder, First grind the liver, then heart, then tongue, then onion, and then garlic.
- Mix and re-grind the mixture once again.
- Add the rest of the ingredients and use your hands to mix it all together.
- Press ingredients into a well-greased bread pan and bake for 45 minutes.
- Prepare the sauce while waiting.
- Add the sauce ingredients in a saucepan and bring it to a boil and pour over the baked meatloaf.

Ghee Cabbage Rice with Lamb
SIBO, WAPF

Ingredients

- 1 tablespoon ghee
- 1 cup cooked rice
- ½ teaspoon chopped ginger
- 1 tablespoon fried onion
- ¼ teaspoon turmeric powder
- 1 cups red cabbage finely chopped
- Salt and pepper to taste
- ½ teaspoon vinegar
- ½ cup grilled lamb steak, cubed

Instructions

- Add very finely chopped red cabbage, ginger, onion, turmeric, and add salt, pepper, and vinegar, and stir fry for 10-15 min until soft.
- Add the cooked rice (see recipe) and lamb cubes.

Grain-Free Mac & Cheese
SIBO

Ingredients

- 8oz Banza Penne Chickpeas pasta
- 1 stick grass-fed butter
- ½ cup cashew flour
- 1 cup grass-fed non-homogenized non-ultrapasturized whole raw milk
- 3 cups sour cream or raw cream fraiche
- 6 cups grated cheddar cheese (or 3 cups cheddar and 3 cups gruyere)
- 1.5 cups coarsely grounded walnuts/ pine nuts in equal amount.
- Salt and pepper to taste

Instructions

- Preheat oven to 350 degrees Farenheit and grease a 9x13" casserole dish.
- Cook the pasta based on the package instruction, drain and set aside.
- Melt the butter under medium low heat, sprinkle the cashew flour and whisk often for 1 minute.
- While whisking, add the milk and cream, and continue cooking under medium low heat until thickened.
- Add 3 cups of the cheese mixture and continue cooking until the cheese is melted . Add salt and pepper to taste.
- Mix the cooked pasta with the sauce and pour inside the casserole dish.
- Sprinkle the top with the remaining 3 cups of cheese and ground walnut and/or pine nuts and bake for 30 minutes.

Green Beans Mushroom Rice

SIBO, WAPF

Ingredients

- 2 cups cooked basmati rice
- 1 tablespoon fried onion
- 1 cup sliced mushrooms, fried in coconut oil until browned
- 1 cup green beans, cut into 1-inch lengths, steamed until dark green
- 3 tablespoons tomato paste
- 2 teaspoon turmeric
- 3 tablespoons coconut oil
- Salt and pepper to taste

Instructions

🍽 Mixed all the ingredients in a pot and heat on low heat for 30 min with the lid closed before serving

Lamb Crown Roast with Bacon Stuffing

GAPS, KETO, PALEO, SIBO, WAPF

Ingredients

- 1 tablespoon rosemary
- 1 tablespoon salt
- 2 teaspoons black pepper
- 5 pounds lamb rib crown roast (about 6 to 7 ribs)

Instructions

- Preheat oven to 375 degrees F.
- Take crown roast of lamb and rub it all over with salt and pepper and rosemary.
- With the ribs on the outside, wrap the rack around onto itself so the ends meet and secure with kitchen twine so it holds its crown shape. Place in a roasting pan.
- Fill the cavity with the Stuffing.
- Cover the stuffing and the tips of the rib bones with foil then place the whole roast in the oven and bake for 1hr, or until an instant-read thermometer inserted near the bone reads 165F.
- 30 min prior to doneness remove the foil to brown the stuffing.
- Remove from the oven, loosely cover with foil and allow to rest for 15 minutes before cutting.

Stuffing

- 2 tablespoons lard
- ½ lb sugar-free bacon
- 1 tablespoon barberries
- 1 tablespoon honey
- 1 cup of shiitaki mushrooms, chopped
- 1 tablespoon fried shallots
- 1 teaspoon fried garlic
- 1 cup sunflower seeds, milled finely
- 1 teaspoon dried thyme
- 1 teaspoon dried sage
- ¼ teaspoon dried chili
- Salt and pepper to taste

Instructions

- 🍽 Sauté the bacon in lard until brown and crispy. Remove the bacon from the skillet and chop to very small pieces. Save the lard to cook the rest of the ingredients in.

- 🍽 Add the honey and barberries to the lard containing skillet and sauté until soft and translucent (about 10 minutes).

- 🍽 Add in the mushrooms and sauté for 5 minutes.

- 🍽 Add the rest of the ingredients and stir for a few minutes while on the stove to mix the flavors.

- 🍽 Stuff the crown roast cavity with this stuffing before putting it in the oven.

Lamb Meatballs and Sautéed Vegetables

GAPS, KETO, PALEO, SIBO, WAPF

Ingredients

Meatballs

- 21 lb ground lamb
- ¼ lb lamb liver, finely chopped
- 2 small shallots, grated
- 1 clove garlic, crushed
- 1 tablespoon, minced ginger
- 1 tablespoon minced turmeric
- 1 tablespoon finely chopped mint
- 1 egg
- ¼ cup Simple Mills grain-free crackers finely processed in a coffee grinder
- 1 tablespoon salt
- 2 teaspoon black pepper
- 1 tablespoon lard

Fried Vegetables

- 2 cups chopped swiss chard
- ½ cup chopped red pepper
- 1 cup chopped yellow zucchini
- ½ cup chopped sugar snaps
- Salt and pepper to taste
- 5-6 tablespoons lard

Instructions

- Mix the meatball ingredients well in a bowl.
- Make small meatballs. If the mixture is runny, use a round spoon and drop a small mass, the size of a meatball on the pan.
- Fry them in 2-3 tablespoons lard for 5 min each side
- Fry the chopped greens and vegetables for 10 min in 2-3 tablespoons lard and add salt and pepper.
- Serve the meatballs on top of fried vegetables

Lamb Miniburgers

GAPS, KETO, PALEO, SIBO, WAPF

Ingredients

- 1 lb ground lamb
- ¼ lb lamb liver, grounded in Omega juicer/grinder, or grated
- 2 small shallots, grounded in omega juicer or grated
- 1 clove garlic, grounded in omega juicer or crushed
- 1 tablespoon, minced ginger, or 1 once cube ginger grounded in omega juicer
- 1 tablespoon minced turmeric or 1 inch cube turmeric root grounded in omega juicer
- 1 tablespoon finely chopped mint, or 2 tablespoon mint leaves, grounded in omega juicer
- 1 egg
- ¼ cup Simple Mills grain-free crackers finely processed in a coffee grinder
- 1 tablespoon salt
- 2 teaspoon black pepper
- 2 cups chopped swiss chard
- ½ cup chopped red pepper
- 1 cup chopped yellow zucchini
- ½ cup chopped sugar snaps
- Salt and pepper to taste
- 2-3 tablespoon lard

Instructions

- Mix the ingredients well in a bowl
- Make small meatballs. If the mixture is runny, use a round spoon and drop a small mass, the size of a meatball on the pan
- Fry them in 1 tablespoon lard for 5 min each side
- Fry the chopped greens and vegetables for 10 min in 2-3 tablespoons lard and add salt and pepper.
- Serve the meatballs on top of fried vegetables

Lamb Pizza
GAPS, KETO, PALEO, SIBO, WAPF

Ingredients

- Cheese
- 1 ¼ cup almond flour
- ¼ cup coconut flour
- ½ teaspoon salt
- 2 duck eggs
- ¼ cup olive oil
- ¼ cup filtered water

Instructions

- Mix the ingredients until sticky dough is formed.
- Place the dough on a parchment paper and place a second paper over the dough. Using a rolling pin flatten the dough into a 14 inch round. Use a pizza cutter to form a smooth crust edge.
- Bake in the oven for 10 min at 350F.

Sauce:

Ingredients

- Mix the ingredients until sticky dough is formed.
- Place the dough on a parchment paper and place a second paper over the dough. Using a rolling pin flatten the dough into a 14 inch round. Use a pizza cutter to form a smooth crust edge.
- Bake in the oven for 10 min at 350F.
- Salt and pepper to taste

Instructions

- Sauté the onion and garlic in beef tallow in high heat until browned.
- Add the diced green bell pepper and sauté for 2-3 minutes.
- Sauté the ground lamb and liver for 5-6 minutes.
- Add the thyme, basil, oregano, salt, pepper
- Add the tomato paste
- Cover the pan and cook for another 10 minutes.
- Remove from the heat and transfer to a deep glass bowl.
- Blend your mixture until it becomes a very smooth paste.
- Paste it evenly over your crust.
- Sprinkle grated cheese generously over it.
- Leave in the oven at 350F for 10 minutes.
- Let it cool down completely before cutting the pizza

Leafy Greens Stew
GAPS, SIBO, WAPF

Ingredients

- 1 lb beef stew meat
- 2 lb chopped spinach
- 1 lb chopped carrot tops
- ½ cup chopped parsley
- ½ cup chopped cilantro
- 3 tablespoons beef tallow
- 2 tablespoon lemon juice, freshly squeezed
- ¼ cup chili beans, soaked in water overnight
- Salt and pepper to taste.

Instructions

- Cook the soaked beans in water under medium heat for about 4hours until soft.
- Put the beef in pot and cover with filtered water.
- Cook on the medium high for 2-3 hours until the meat is soft and then add the cooked beans to the pot.
- In the meantime, fry the greens with the beef tallow on medium high until their color turns dark green, about 20min.
- Add the green the meat pot and add lemon juice and salt and pepper to taste.
- Let simmer in medium heat for 15-20 minutes.

Mushroom Culiflower Curry

GAPS, KETO, PALEO, SIBO, WAPF

Ingredients

- 2 cups red, yellow, and white cauliflower, broken into tiny florets
- 3 tablespoons coconut oil
- 1 tablespoon fried onion
- ½ tablespoon crushed garlic
- 1 cup chopped equal amount of shiitake, oyster, enoki, and wood ear mushrooms, fried
- 1 tablespoon curry
- 1 tablespoon garam masala
- ½ cup coconut cream
- Salt and pepper to taste

Instructions

- In a large pan, toss the cauliflower florets in coconut oil, and season with salt and pepper, cover with a lid and cook on low heat for 15-20min until the florets are softened.
- Add all the ingredients and spices and stir thoroughly and cook for another 10-15 min on low heat.

Mushroom Root Vegetable Patties

GAPS, SIBO, WAPF

Ingredients

- ¼ cup equal amount of oyster, enoki, and shitaki mushrooms, chopped
- 1 cup root vegetables (turnip, rutabaga, celeriac), chopped
- 2 tablespoons olive oil
- ½ teaspoon turmeric
- 2 eggs
- 3 tablespoon coconut oil
- Salt and pepper to taste

Instructions

- Put the roasted vegetables in a pyrex dish, add olive oil, turmeric, salt, and pepper. Roast the root vegetables in the oven at 400F for 45 min.
- Let the root vegetables cool down. Then process it with the mushrooms and eggs in a food processor for a few minutes until it becomes a smooth paste.
- Make small patties, either elongated or round hamburger shape and fry them in coconut oil.

Mushroom Zucchini Lasagna

GAPS, SIBO, WAPF

Ingredients

- 3-4 tablespoon duck fat for frying
- 1 tablespoon chopped garlic
- 2 tablespoon chopped onion
- 1 ¼ cup mushrooms, sliced
- 1 cup chopped red/yellow, orange, green bell peppers
- 1 jar 6 oz tomato paste
- 1 tablespoon fresh chopped basil
- 1 tablespoon fresh chopped parsley
- 1 tablespoon fresh chopped cilantro
- Salt and pepper to taste
- 2 large zucchini, sliced thinly
- 1 pkg of 8oz organic shredded mozzarella cheese

Instructions

- Preheat oven to 350 degree farenheit.
- Fry garlic and onion until translucent.
- Add in mushrooms and sauté for 10 minutes.
- Add in bell peppers and sauté for 5 minutes. Stir in tomato paste.
- Add in the herbs, salt and pepper, continue to stir for a few more minutes.
- Grease a 9" x 13" baking dish with duck fat.
- Place a thin layer (½ inch) of the sauce in the baking dish.
- Layer zucchini and mushrooms/bell peppers over sauce, and repeat, alternating layering of sauce, then zucchini and mushrooms/bell peppers.
- Top off with a layer of cheese. Bake lasagna for 30 minutes until the cheese melts.

Organ Meat Hot Pocket
GAPS, KETO, PALEO, SIBO

Preheat the oven to 350 degrees.

Prepare the Crust:
- Whisk together the following dry ingredients
  » 2 ¼ cup almond flour
  » 2 tablespoons Coconut Flour
  » ½ teaspoon baking Soda
  » 1 teaspoon dried rosemary
  » 1 teaspoon turmeric
  » ½ teaspoon sea salt

Add the following wet ingredients
- 3 large eggs
- 2 tablespoons melted ghee
- ½ teaspoon saffron
- Beat together until frothy and pour in the middle of the dry ingredients. Mix until dough is formed.

Filling
- 1 tablespoon tallow
- 1 tablespoon chopped lamb kidney (fat removed)
- 2 tablespoons chopped lamb heart (fat and heart valves removed)
- ½ cup ground dark turkey
- 1 tablespoon fried onions
- 1/2 tablespoons fried garlic
- 1/2 teaspoon thyme
- 1/2 teaspoon chipotle chili pepper
- A dash of cayenne pepper
- Salt and black pepper to taste

Filling preparation

- For the filling preparation, oil the pan and mix all the ingredients. Cook for 20 minutes on medium heat until the meat is browned. Using a handheld blender, blend your mixture to a smooth paste.

- Cut a small piece of dough about 1inch in diameter and roll into an even ball and place it on top of a piece of parchment paper from Amazon. Top with another piece of parchment paper and roll the dough 1/2" thick. Remove the top piece of parchment paper.

- Oil your hands with coconut oil to prevent the dough sticking to your hands.

- To make the pizza pockets, place one tablespoon of the filling in the middle of the circle of dough. Fold dough from the top over filling; firmly press edges to seal tightly.

- Place the pockets in the oven for 20 minutes.

Persian Chicken Kabob
GAPS, KETO, PALEO, SIBO, WAPF

Ingredients

- 1 lb chicken thigh, cut in 1 cubic inches
- ½ cup chopped onion
- ½ teaspoon saffron
- 2 teaspoon salt
- 2 tablespoons freshly squeezed lime juice
- 2 tablespoons olive oil

Instructions

- Marinade the chicken with the rest of the ingredients and leave in the refrigerator for a few hours to overnight
- Put each six piece on a long skewer.
- On the grill, remove the top and place the ends of the skewer on the two ends of the grill width-wise.
- Turn on the grill and rotate the skewer every few minutes to prevent burning of the meat, until the meat is cooked, about 15-20min.
- Serve over cooked rice.

Persian Saffron Berberis Cauli-rice

GAPS, KETO, PALEO, SIBO, WAPF

Ingredients

- 1 medium size cauliflower, chopped to small florets
- ½ cup berberries
- ¼ teaspoon saffron in 1oz hot water
- ½ cup honey
- 3 tablespoons ghee
- Salt and pepper to taste

Instructions

- Process the cauliflower florets in a Breville processor until it looks like rice grains.
- Add 3 tablespoons ghee on a large saucepan, add the cauliflower and salt cover and cook for 20 minutes.
- Sauté the barberries in honey and ghee for 10 min until translucent.
- Put the cauli-rice on a serving plate and decorate the top with saffron and sautéed barberries.

Pork Crown Roast with Bacon Stuffing

GAPS, KETO, PALEO, SIBO, WAPF

Ingredients

- 1 tablespoon rosemary
- 1 tablespoon Salt
- 2 teaspoons black pepper
- 10 pounds pork rib crown roast (about 12 to 14 ribs)

Instructions

- Preheat oven to 375 degrees F. Take crown roast of pork and Rub the pork all over with salt and pepper and rosemary. With the ribs on the outside, wrap the rack around onto itself so the ends meet and secure with kitchen twine so it holds its crown shape. Place in a roasting pan.

- Fill the cavity with the Stuffing. Cover the stuffing and the tips of the rib bones with foil then place the whole roast in the oven and bake for 2 hours and 20 minutes, an instant-read thermometer inserted near the bone should register 165 degrees F when done. About 30 to 45 minutes prior to doneness, remove the foil to brown the stuffing and create a crust. Remove from the oven, loosely cover with foil and allow to rest for 30 minutes before cutting.

Stuffing:

Ingredients

- 2 tablespoons lard
- ½ lb sugar-free bacon
- 1 tablespoon berberries or cranberries
- 1 tablespoon honey
- 1 cup of shiitaki mushrooms, chopped
- 1 tablespoon fried shallots (see recipe)
- 1 teaspoon fried garlic (see recipe)
- 1 cup sunflower seeds, milled finely
- 1 teaspoon dried thyme
- 1 teaspoon dried sage
- ¼ teaspoon dried chili
- Salt and pepper to taste

Instructions

- Sauté the bacon in lard until brown and crispy. Remove the bacon from the skillet and chop to very small pieces. Save the lard to cook the rest of the ingredients in.
- Add the honey and barberries to the lard containing skillet and sauté until soft and translucent (about 10 minutes).
- Add in the mushrooms and sauté for 5 minutes.
- Add the rest of the ingredients and stir for a few minutes while on the stove to mix the flavors.
- Stuff the crown roast cavity with this stuffing before putting it in the oven.

Rotisserie Goose
GAPS, KETO, PALEO, SIBO, WAPF

Ingredients

- 27 lb fresh goose
- 2-3 tablespoon salt
- 1 tablespoon pepper
- Deep roasting pan

Instructions

- Preheat the oven to 400F.
- Warm the goose to room temperature for a few hours prior. Season the goose inside the cavity and out all over the skin with salt and pepper.
- Fill out the bird's cavity with the filling.
- Place the goose on the rack in the pan and cover with the lid. Cook for 30 min and reduce the heat to 325F.
- Roast the bird for 5 hours with the lid closed, and 30 min to 1 extra hour with the lid open to brown the skin or until instant-read thermometer inserted into the thickest part of the thigh reads 165 F.
- Take the pan out, cover with the lid, and wait for 15 minutes before serving.

Filling inside the cavity

- 4 tablespoons Ghee
- 4 medium Granny Smith apples, skinned, cored, and thinly sliced
- 2 garlic cloves, crushed
- 1 cup pecan halves, milled
- ¼ c. fresh parsley, finely chopped
- 2 tablespoon. fresh mint, finely chopped
- ¼ cup pomegranate seeds
- 1 tablespoon fried onion
- Salt and pepper to taste

Instructions

- 🍽 Sauté the apples in ghee for 5 minute.
- 🍽 Add the rest of the ingredients and sauté for another 5 minutes.
- 🍽 Stuff the bird's cavity with it before putting it in the oven.

Turkey Meatballs
GAPS, KETO, PALEO, SIBO, WAPF

Ingredients

- 1 lb ground dark turkey
- ¼ lb turkey liver, grounded in Omega Juicer
- 2 small shallots, grounded in Omega juicer or grated
- 1 clove garlic, grounded in omega juicer or crushed
- 1 tablespoon, minced ginger, or 1 once cube ginger grounded in omega juicer
- 1 tablespoon minced turmeric or 1 inch cube turmeric root grounded in omega juicer
- 1 tablespoon finely chopped mint, or 2 tablespoon mint leaves, grounded in omega juicer
- 1 egg
- ¼ cup Simple Mills grain-free crackers finely processed in a coffee grinder
- 1 tablespoon salt
- 2 teaspoon black pepper
- 2 cups chopped Kale
- 1 cup finely chopped green beans
- ½ cup chopped carrots
- 2-3 tablespoon lard.

Instructions

- 🍽 Mix the ingredients well in a bowl
- 🍽 Make small meatballs. If the mixture is runny, use a round spoon and drop a small mass, the size of a meatball on the pan
- 🍽 Fry them in 1 tablespoon lard for 5 min each side
- 🍽 Fry the chopped greens and vegetables for 10 min in 2-3 tablespoons lard and add salt and pepper.
- 🍽 Serve the meatballs on top of fried vegetables

Snack Food

Raw Peanut Walnut Bar

GAPS, KETO, PALEO, SIBO, WAPF

Ingredients

- 2 cups moist medjool dates, pitted, skinned and chopped
- 2 cups raw peanut
- ½ cup raw walnut
- ¾ cup non-alkalized cocoa powder
- ½ cup unsweetened shredded coconuts
- 2 tablespoon vanilla extract
- 2 tablespoon peanut butter

Instructions

- Combine chopped dates, peanuts, walnuts, and cocoa powder in a food processor.
- Pulse and process all the ingredients together until the texture is coarse.
- Add the shredded coconut, a quick pulse, and add the vanilla extract, add peanut butter one tablespoon at a time until it reaches a dry but moist dough consistency.
- Scrape the dough mixture into the lined 9"x11" pan, press evenly with a rubber spatula or your clean hands, and chill in the refrigerator for about an hour before cutting them in 16 equal rectangle servings.

Raw Super Nuts & Roasted Super Seeds Energy Bars

GAPS, PALEO, SIBO, WAPF

Ingredients

- ½ cup raisins
- ½ cup dates
- 2 tablespoon 5-seed butter by Beyond the Equator
- 2 teaspoon vanilla extract
- 2.5 cups mixed nuts (cashews, brazil nuts, macademia nuts)
- 2 tablespoon of shredded coconut

Instructions

- In a bowl, add all ingredients, except the mixed nut, and process until it forms a ball-like paste. Add the mixed nuts pulsing a few times to just cut up some of the nuts.

- Press the mix into a quarter sheet silicon baking mar, spreading it out evenly. Refrigerate for about 1 hour, then cut up into 3'x2' squares and enjoy as a breakfast to go.

Dessert

Butternut Squash Bars
GAPS, PALEO, SIBO, WAPF

Ingredients

- 2 ½ cups roasted and mashed butternut squash
- ¼ cup cashews
- ¼ cup coconut butter (or shredded coconut)
- 2 tablespoon coconut flour
- ½ tablespoon cinnamon
- 1 teaspoon crushed fresh ginger roots
- 3 tablespoon honey
- ¼ cup coconut oil

Instructions

- Preheat the oven to 400 degrees.
- Cut the butternut squash in half, remove seeds and place face down on a baking sheet. Bake 45 minutes, or until it's soft enough when pierced with a knife.
- Once it's cooled, scoop the meaty part of the squash into the blender.
- Put the rest of the ingredients in a blender and blend until a smooth paste is formed.
- Oil a large pyrex dish with coconut oil and pour in the mixture in.
- Let it bake for 45 minutes at 375 degrees.
- Let it cool down before cutting it to square shaped bars.

Optional:

- Top with shredded coconut or sliced almonds before baking.

Butternut Squash Bread

GAPS, PALEO, SIBO, WAPF

Ingredients

- 1 ½ cup roasted and mashed butternut squash
- ¼ cup coconut oil
- ¼ cup honey
- 1 teaspoon vanilla extract
- 1 cup walnut flour
- ½ cup coconut flour
- ½ teaspoon baking soda
- ½ teaspoon cinnamon
- A pinch of salt

Instructions

- Preheat the oven to 400 degrees.
- Cut the butternut squash in half, remove seeds and place face down on a baking sheet.
- Bake 45 minutes, or until it's soft enough when pierced with a knife.
- Lower oven temperature to 350 degrees.
- Once it's cooled, scoop the meaty part of the squash and mix with the wet ingredients using a blender.
- Mix dry ingredients together
- Add dry ingredients into wet mixture. Mix well.
- Pour into greased 9x5inch loaf pan and bake for 45 minutes.

Cheesecake Pie
SIBO, WAPF

Ingredients

- 1 (9 inch) prepared organic spelt pie shell
- 1 cup cream cheese (2x8oz packages)
- ½ cup coconut sugar
- 2 eggs
- 1 teaspoons vanilla extract
- 1 cup sour cream

Instructions

- Preheat oven to 350 degrees F.
- Mix all the ingredients.
- Bake for 1hr until the top is set.
- After it cooled down, place it in refrigerator for 2h before serving.
- Top with raw whipcream

Chia Seed Pudding

GAPS, PALEO, SIBO, WAPF

Ingredients

- 1 cup coconut cream
- ¼ cup chia seed
- ¼ cup maple syrup
- 1 tablespoon vanilla
- 1 cup Paleonola (grain-free granola)

Instructions

- Mix the ingredients and refrigerate for 2 hours
- Top with paleonola and serve.

Einkorn Cupcakes
SIBO, WAPF

Ingredients

- ½ cup almond flour
- ½ cup einkorn flour
- ¼ cup coconut flour
- 1 teaspoon salt
- ½ teaspoon baking soda
- 8 large eggs
- 1 stick melted butter butter
- 4 tablespoons raw honey
- 1 tablespoon vanilla extract

Instructions

- Preheat the oven to 330F.
- Place paper baking cups in each of the 12 regular size muffin cups.
- Combine the salt, almond flour, Einkorn flour, coconut flour and baking soda in a large bowl. In a medium bowl, whisk together the eggs, butter, honey, and vanilla.
- With a handheld blender, blend the wet ingredients with the dry ingredients until thoroughly combined.
- Bake for 30-35 minutes. Once inserted toothpick comes out clean, the cupcakes are ready.
- Frost after the cupcakes are cooled down.

Frosting

- ½ cup homemade raw cream fraiche (see recipe)
- 3 tablespoons honey
- 1-tablespoon vanilla extract

Instructions

- 🍽 Mix all the ingredients and whip with a whisker until the cream can hold a stiff peak.
- 🍽 Keep in the refrigerator until ready to use.

Paleona Butter Cake

GAPS, PALEO, WAPF

Ingredients

- 3 cups grain-free Paleona
- 1.5 teaspoon baking soda
- 1 cup salted butter
- 4 large eggs
- 1 cup coconut milk
- Sunbutter frosting
- ½ cup honey
- ½ cup sunflower butter
- 1 teaspoon vanilla extract

Instructions

- Preheat oven to 350 degrees and grease and flour a 9x13 Baking pan.
- Ground Paleona in a grinder until smooth
- Whisk together the grounded paleona and baking soda.
- Melt the butter. Mix in eggs one at a time
- Add the coconut milk.
- Add dry mixture to butter mixture.
- Pour batter into the pan and bake for 45 minutes.
- Mix the ingredients for sunbutter frosting.
- After cake is removed from oven, let the cake cool for about 10 minutes and then remove from pan before it gets too cold and stick to the pan.
- Add the frosting to the top of the cake.

Persimmon Pie
WAPF

Ingredients

- ½ cup almond flour
- ½ cup Einkorn flour

For Filling

- 2 cups of blended ripe persimmons (about 7-9 medium size)
- 3 eggs
- 4 tablespoons honey
- 2 teaspoons cinnamon
- ¼ teaspoon cloves
- ¼ teaspoon allspice
- ¼ teaspoon nutmeg
- ½ teaspoon cardamom
- 1 teaspoon natural vanilla

Instructions

- Preheat oven to 325.
- Mix crust ingredients by hand in a bowl.
- Press crust into bottom and sides of a well-greased pie pan and put in the oven for 10min.
- Combine the filling ingredients and mix with a Cuisinart hand blender.
- Pour the filling over the crust and return to oven for an hour or until center is no longer wet.
- Top with Dang unsweetened toasted coconut chips and/or Bare apple chips.

Pumpkin Bars
GAPS, PALEO, SIBO, WAPF

Ingredients

- 2 medium-sized Kent pumpkins
- ½ tablespoon cardamom
- ½ tablespoon cinnamon
- 1 teaspoon all spice
- 1 teaspoon cloves
- 1 teaspoon crushed fresh ginger roots
- 4 ripened bananas
- 2 tablespoon honey
- ½ cup coconut oil
- 8 eggs

Instructions

- Preheat the oven to 400 degrees.
- Bake the whole pumpkins for 1 hour. Turn off the oven and let them stay in the oven for several hours until it's cooled down.
- Remove the seeds and scoop the meaty part of the pumpkin into the blender.
- Put the rest of the ingredients in a blender and blend until a smooth paste is formed.
- Oil a large Pyrex dish with coconut oil and pour in the mixture in.
- Let it bake for 1 hour at 400 degrees.
- Let it cool down before cutting it to square shaped bars.

Before serving (optional):

- Mix equal 1 tablespoon honey and 1 tablespoon Tahini and spread on top of each bar.

Pumpkin Cupcakes
GAPS, PALEO, SIBO, WAPF

Ingredients

- 1 package of Simple mills grain-free pumpkin cupcake mix
- 3 eggs
- 1 cup water
- 3 tablespoon melted butter

Frosting

- 1 cup smooth peanut butter
- 1 tablespoon vanilla extract
- 2 tablespoon raw honey

Instructions

- 🍽 Make the cupcakes following the package instructions.
- 🍽 For frosting, mix all the ingredients and mix thoroughly. frost the cupcakes and add one blueberry on top.

Pupped Quinoa Chocolate

Ingredients

- ¼ cup refined coconut oil, melted
- ¼ cup cocoa butter, melted
- ¼ cup maple syrup
- ¼ cup cocoa powder
- 1 teaspoon vanilla extract
- 1 ½ cup popped quinoa

Instructions

- In a bowl mix all ingredients together and fold in the popped quinoa at the end.
- Leave in the refrigerator for 1 hour until harden.
- Cut square pieces and serve.

Sweet Potato Paleonola Cupcakes
GAPS, SIBO, WAPF

Ingredients

- One large sweet potatoes baked and pureed (16oz)
- 1 cup salted butter, melted and cooled
- 1 cup honey
- 4 large eggs
- 2 cups grinded paleonola
- 2 teaspoon baking soda
- 2 teaspoons ground cinnamon
- 1 teaspoon pumpkin spice

Instructions

- Preheat the oven to 350 degrees F. Line a cupcake pan with 18 paper liners, set aside.
- In a large bowl, mix the wet ingredients with an electric mixer until completely uniform.
- Add the dry ingredients and whisk until it forms a smooth batter.
- Fill each cupcake in the prepared pan three-quarters full of batter.
- Bake for 25 minutes. Let it cool.
- Frost the cupcakes with raw cream fraiche and fresh berries.

Author's Bio:

Dr Nakisa Nowroozi is passionate about promoting the concept of "food as medicine" and is eager to educate families about the real healthy living.

Nakisa has a Master's degree in Biochemistry and a doctorate degree in the field of cell and molecular biology. Because of her extensive academic and professional background, Nakisa is able to extract nutritional research information and distinguish between real and fake science and determine if a claim regarding the nutritional benefits of a food is true or not. In March 2020, Nakisa founded Nourishality Superfood Snacks to help families with nutrient-dense on-the-go sprouted supersnacks that are easy on the gut.

www.nourishality.com

Made in the USA
Coppell, TX
22 June 2022

79122260R00066